TEACH YOURSELF PRAISE GUITAR

Teach Yourself
PRAISE GUITAR

JO KING

KINGSWAY PUBLICATIONS
EASTBOURNE

ISBN 0 86065 228 9

Scripture quotations are from the
New International Version, copyright © New
York International Bible
Society 1978

S. of F. refers to the *Songs of Fellowship* songbooks.

Printed in Great Britain for
KINGSWAY PUBLICATIONS LTD
Lottbridge Drove, Eastbourne, E. Sussex BN23 6NT by
Stanley L. Hunt (Printers) Ltd, Rushden, Northants.
Typeset by Nuprint Services Ltd, Harpenden, Herts.

CONTENTS

PART TWO: LEADING WORSHIP

Part One
Learning to Strum

LESSON 1

1. The guitar

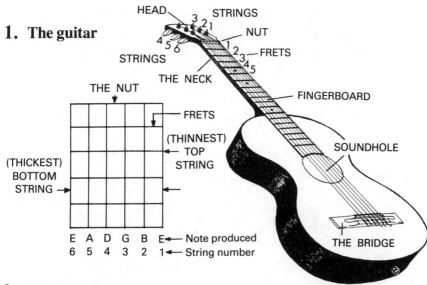

2. How to tune up

(a) If you have a piano and know which note is middle C, then your 6th string (bottom E) is the note nearly 2 octaves below middle C. A tuning fork or a pitch pipe is another means of obtaining a note to which you can tune your guitar. If none of these are at hand, listen to your cassette and tune your 6th string to the note given there.

(b) Count 5 spaces up the neck of the guitar, starting at the *nut* (which counts as 0, not 1). Place your finger firmly on the E string (6th) just behind the 5th fret. The note it gives you is the note to which the A string (5th) has to be tuned.

7

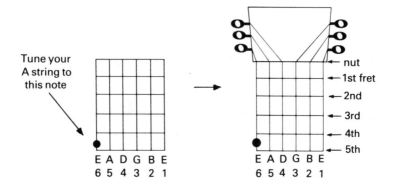

Tune your
A string to
this note

E A D G B E
6 5 4 3 2 1

nut
1st fret
2nd
3rd
4th
5th

E A D G B E
6 5 4 3 2 1

(c) Repeat the process with the A and D strings, and the D and G strings.

(d) In the case of the G and B strings, count 4 spaces up the neck along the G string, placing your finger firmly behind the 4th fret. The note it gives you is the note to which the B string has to be tuned.

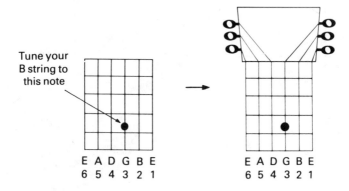

Tune your
B string to
this note

E A D G B E
6 5 4 3 2 1

E A D G B E
6 5 4 3 2 1

(e) For the B and E strings, count 5 spaces up, placing your finger firmly behind the 5th fret on the B string. This is the note for the top E string.

3. Fingering

A simple system of fingering will be used throughout this book. The fingers of the *left hand* will be numbered 1 to 5, thumb to little finger.

4. Chords

All chords for the songs used throughout this book can be found on page 43 at the end of Part 1. They will be denoted like this:

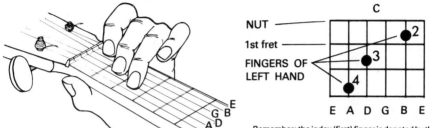

Remember: the index (first) finger is denoted by the number 2. The number 1 is reserved for the thumb, which can sometimes be used.

5. The capo

You may find that a particular song sounds good in say, the key of G, but that then it is too low for people to sing. By simply affixing the *capo* onto the fingerboard you will still be able to play in G and the melody will now be in a comfortable range for your voice.

What the capo is doing is effectively moving the 'nut' up the neck of the guitar. For every fret you move up, you raise the sound of the chord you play by one semitone. So, for example, if you play G on capo 1, you get A♭; if you play Em on capo 2, you get F♯m.

Some songbooks give you a capo setting so that you can play easier chord shapes while remaining in tune with the piano—see *Songs of Fellowship* no. 62 as an example.

The use of the capo will be indicated in this book as required: thus 'capo 2' simply means that the capo is to be placed between the 1st and 2nd frets.

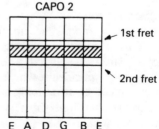

CAPO 2

E A D G B E

Here for example is the chord of G,
capo 1.

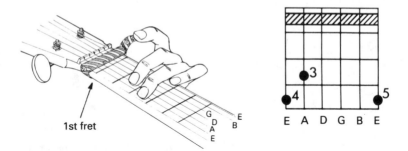

1st fret

E A D G B E

6. The plectrum

I find the large, thin plectrums to my personal liking, but this may not be so in your case. Hold the plectrum *loosely* between the 2nd and 3rd fingers on one side and the thumb on the other, so that approximately half the plectrum is covered.

Important note
The sign > means 'accented stroke'. When the words and chords are given for a song this sign will appear over the words to indicate where the accents are to be played. The diagrams on strumming in each lesson will show more specifically where those accents come. The accents are not to be produced by strumming harder, but rather by a sharper movement of the wrist. Without them, your strumming is in danger of becoming monotonous.

7. Here is the song *I Will Enter His Gates* (Capo 1) (*S.o.F. no. 62*).
As your chorded vocabulary increases more luscious chords can be
added, but first of all we need to provide a basic chordal structure.

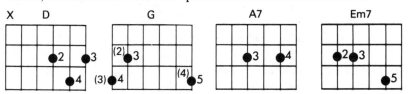

Key: X means 'don't play that string'. The bracketed numbers are alternative
fingerings.

```
1 + 2 + 3 + 4 + | 1 + 2 + 3 + 4 + | 1 + 2 + 3 + 4  + | 1 + 2 + 3  +  4   +   |
                |   D       A7    |  G         D     |  D        G          |
                |   >  >  >  >  > |  >  >  >  >   >   |  >   >     >      >   |
                                               I will | enter His gates with thanks─ |
```

D >   >   >   > | >   > G   >   >| A7 >   >   >
giving in my heart, I will | enter His courts with | praise,

        > | D   >   > G >   > | D >   >   >
I will | say this is the day that the | Lord has made,

>   {Em7   >   >   A7   >   > | D > > > >
I {G   >
I | will rejoice for He has made me | glad.

        >   > G > > | D   >   >   >
He has made me glad, | He has made me glad,

> {Em7   >   >   A7 >   > | D > > > >
I {G   >
I | will rejoice for He has made me | glad.

        >   > G >   > | D   >   >   >
He has made me glad, | He has made me glad,

> {Em7 >   >   A7   >   > | D > >   >
I {G
I | will rejoice for He has made me | glad.

Note: The { brackets around chords show alternatives: thus here either
Em7 or G can be used.

8. Changing chords

(a) Placement of fingers for the chord of D. If the fingers are much further away from the frets than is shown here, an unpleasant buzzing sound is likely to occur.

(b) Make sure the wrist and the fingers are arched over the strings, or else one or two of the strings may be stopped from vibrating.

(c) Use the *tips* of the fingers to produce a mellow tone.

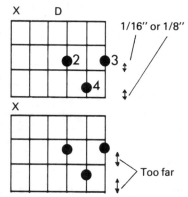

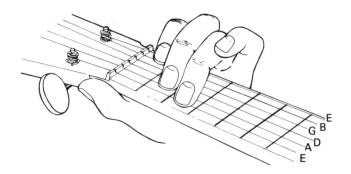

(d) Make sure the fingernails of your left hand are cut short or buzzing might result.

9. Pivot notes

You will notice in looking at the fingering for both Em7 and A7 (see the chord chart on page 43) that there is a finger common to both chords. Therefore this finger doesn't have to leave its position while the move from Em7 to A7 is being executed. This makes for greater economy of movement as you play Em7 and your hand swivels round on your 3rd finger ready to bring your 4th finger down onto the B string for A7.

In future lessons we will see similar moves under the heading *Pivot notes*.

LESSON 2

1. Strumming

These lessons are geared to making your strumming technique interesting, so that for a particular song you're not just moving your hand up and down in haphazard fashion. You need to be aware of all the strokes you use and in complete control of them.

Strumming is given character by a contrast of accented and light strokes.

If you hold the plectrum loosely between your fingers and strum, this will give you a light sound. If you want to incorporate accents into this, then a sharper action of the wrist must be used.

Also, there is a tendency when starting to strum to be timid in your approach. Keep a free action in your wrist and a fairly large arc as you strum.The smaller the arc, the more timid and tense you are likely to sound.

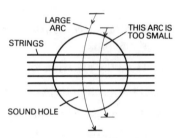

2. On pages 47–48 there are 7 lists of songs, each list representing one particular strumming pattern. So, for example, once you've mastered the strumming for *I Will Enter His Gates* you will be able to use that strumming for all the songs in List 1.

3. The strumming pattern for *I Will Enter His Gates* is:

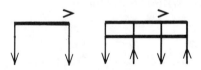

This diagram may look very involved at first sight, but here is a key to help you understand it.

↓ means a down-stroke

↑ means an up-stroke

> means accent that stroke

⌐ is equivalent to ⌐⌐ in duration. So, for example, here is the strumming pattern on page 13, showing how many strokes go to make up each beat.

4.

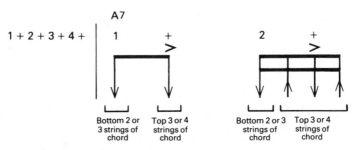

5. (i) Contrast accented strokes and light strokes – produces interesting strumming.

(ii) Hold the plectrum loosely – produces light strumming.

(iii) Sharp action from a relaxed wrist – produces accents.

(iv) Practise slowly at first – produces controlled playing.

(v) Constantly try to *relax* – produces smooth playing.

LESSON 3

Changing chords while strumming

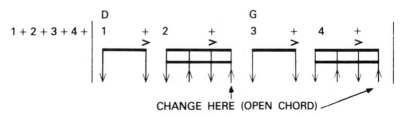

Note
'Open chord' means that on the stroke indicated no fingers are touching the strings. The fingers have momentarily left the fingerboard on their way to a new chord. (This is demonstrated on the tape.)

14

LESSON 4

1. Before moving on to another type of strumming, let's consolidate on the present one by looking at the next song in list 1 on page 47, *For I'm Building a People of Power* (Capo 1) (*S.o.F. no. 25*). So as not to give you the extra task of learning a whole set of new chords, I've kept it in the same key as the previous song.

There is only one new chord, D7.

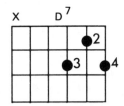

```
1 + 2 + 3 + 4 + | 1 + 2 + 3 + 4 + | 1 + 2 + 3 +  4   + | 1 +  2   +  3  + 4 + |
                     >   >  >   >       >   >  >      >      D    >   > G  >   >
                   D       G         D       A7         building a people of
                                           For I'm |
```

```
D >     >    >            > { Em7          > A7>      > | D  >   >   >
                             { A7 >
power             And I'm | making a people of | praise,
```

```
     >           >          >  G >     > | D  >   >   >
That will | move through this land by My | Spirit,
```

```
      >        { Em7 > A7>        >   | D  >   > (D7) >
      >        { A7 >
And will | glorify My precious | Name.
```

```
        >   | G     >     > (A7) >     > | D   >     >   >
Build Your | Church, Lord,     make us | strong, Lord,
```

```
       >    { Em7  >      >(A7)>        >  | D  >  > (D7) >
       >    { A7
Join our | hearts, Lord,     through Your | Son.
```

```
        >  | G    >     >(A7) >     >  | D>   >   >
Make us | one, Lord,     in Your | Body,
```

```
       >  { Em7 >     A7 >     >  | D  >  >  >
       >  { A7 >
In the | kingdom     of Your | Son.
```

15

2. You will notice that there are some chords in round brackets. These chords are optional extras. Their omission will not detract from the whole effect, but their insertion will add a little colour to the music.

As in the previous song, the bracketed chords $\begin{Bmatrix} \text{Em7} \\ \text{A7} \end{Bmatrix}$ constitute an instruction to use *either* Em7 *or* A7, though the insertion of Em7 will add a little more flavour than simply playing A7.

HOW TO PRACTISE: VITAL PRINCIPLES

Many people practise without any kind of method. Each time they pick up the guitar they have little idea how best to use their time. When mistakes start cropping up they don't really overcome them and so eventually they end up practising mistakes. Over a lengthy period of time bad habits become ingrained and difficult to remove.

Here are some ways of making economic use of your practice time.

Some principles of practice

(a) Sectionalize the song. Thus, in your first practice session on *I Will Enter His Gates,* look at the section from the beginning up to 'He has made me glad'. In your second practice session look at the section from 'He has made me glad' to the end.

(b) Go through the first section isolating all the moves, D to G, G to D, G to A7, A7 to D, and so on. Practise the first chord change, strumming the first chord once and letting it resonate. If the strings buzz then your fingers are probably not close enough to the frets.

Now look at what fingers are to be used for the next chord and whereabouts they are to be placed.

Strum the strings again and, as you move to this next chord, make sure you don't stop the strings from resonating. If you do, you'll have a gap between the first and second chords.

Only when you've got the first chord change moving smoothly must you move on.

Don't concentrate on the strumming while you're learning the chord shapes and changes. It will only confuse matters.

When you've got these individual moves a little smoother, try linking the moves together in groups, for example D to G to A7 as one group. Then D to G to A7 to D, and so on.

(c) Now try the same moves without looking at the fingers of your left hand. This will help you to play by *touch* rather than sight. It will also

17

show up the weaker fingers. When you get a particular move wrong, look at the fingers, repeating the exercise correctly. Then repeat it without looking.

(d) Next, concentrate on the strumming. Try out the strumming on two chords at first, remembering to:
(i) Start at a speed which is comfortably slow for you.
(ii) Keep that speed regular, no matter how slow.
(iii) Resist the temptation to hesitate on strumming while changing chords. If you falter while changing chords this may turn into a habit that is difficult to correct. It may help if you reduce speed so that you can change without faltering.
(iv) Use the *open chord* technique in lesson 3.
(v) Connect chords—don't stop the strings resonating while changing chords.

(e) Don't waste time playing sections of the song you can do well when there are still parts of the song you're struggling with.

(f) You may find that, on coming back to play a certain section you thought you'd conquered the day before, it starts to fall apart and seems to get worse.

When returning to look at a passage you previously thought you'd sewn up, always start practising *slowly*. If you start playing it at performance speed, you're likely to make a number of slips and jump to the conclusion – wrongly – that you didn't practise properly the last time.

(g) Rather than practise for one hour, break the time into two half-hour sessions. When you know you've got a long time to practise, your concentration is not likely to be as good as when you've only got half the time.

Especially as a beginner, it's no use practising till your hand and fingers are aching and sore. It is better to have a few short intense sessions.

LESSON 5

1. *Hallelujah, for the Lord Our God* (capo 3) *(S.o.F. no. 30).*

```
1 + 2 + 3 + 4 + | 1 + 2 + 3 + 4 + | 1 + 2 + 3 + 4   + | 1 + 2  + 3 + 4   +
                |  D       G      |  D       A7       |  D
                |    >  >  >  >   |    >  >  >    >    |    >     >  >    >
                |                 |           Halle lu-jah,      for the
```

```
 G    >   > D >   >  {Em7 > > > A7 > | D  >  >    >     >  } Halle lu —
 Lord our God the Al migh—— ty     | reigns. ——      |
                      A7
```

```
  >   >    >  | G   >   > D >   > {Em7 > > > > | D  >  >
 jah,     for the| Lord our God the Al migh——— ty | reigns. ——
                                    A7
```

```
   >    >  |G >    >  >   >  | D > > >    > | E7  > >     >    >
 Let us re joi ——ce and be | gla — d And | give the glory unto
```

```
 A7 >   >   >    > | D >      >   >    > | G   >   > D >
 Him. —— Halle lu ——jah,   for the | Lord our God
```

```
    >  |{Em7 > > > A7 > | D  >   >   >
 The Al migh——— ty    | reigns. ——
         A7
```

The only new chord to learn here is E7.

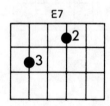

2. Pivot notes

Em7 to A7 (3rd finger).

3. We could go through all the remaining songs in list 1, but it would take up valuable time which needs to be spent in looking at other types of strumming. So let's move on.

19

LESSON 6

1. This lesson introduces you to a new strumming pattern. All the songs in list 2 on page 47 can be played with it. Let's look at the first song in that list, *We Are More Than Conquerors*.

```
1   2   3   4 | 1   2   3   4 | 1   2   3   4 | 1   2   3   4 |
              | G             | {Am7          | D7            |
              |     >     >   | {Am >      >  |     >      >  |
```

```
1   2   3   4 | 1   2                        {Am7            D7
G       C     | G   >              >         {Am              
    >      >  |   We are more than | conquerors,   >      >  |  >        >    |
              |                               >      >       | Overcomers in this |
```

```
G   (C)  G                            {Am7
  >    >   >                 >        {Am  >      >
  life.   | We've been made vic|torious        |
```

```
D7  >                  >     | G    >  (C) >  |  G
  By the blood of Jesus | Christ.            |    >
```

Here are the new chords:

Am

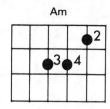

Am⁷

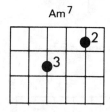

C

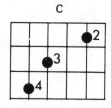

2. Here is the strumming for this song:

```
1   +   2   +   3   +   4   +  | 1        +          2        +
                              | G
```

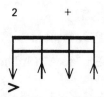

20

3.

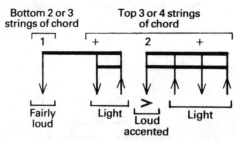

Here is a graph to help you visualize the contrast in volume for each stroke.

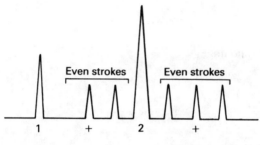

4. This is a diagram showing the first 2 strokes you make in this type of strumming.

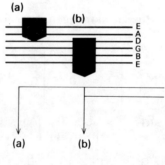

$1 + 2 + 3 + 4 +$

CHANGE HERE (open chord)

5. Also practise: { Am7 / Am } to D7, D7 to G, G to C, and C to G.

21

6. If you find the above diagram a little difficult to understand, the following may help you.

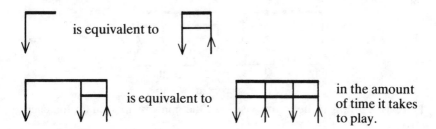

7. Pivot notes

$\begin{cases} \text{Am7} \\ \text{Am} \end{cases}$ to D7 (2nd finger)

LESSON 7

1. Here is the second song from the list on page 47, *I Love You, Lord (S.o.F. no. 49).*

```
1   2   3   4 |1   2   3   4 |1   2   3   4 |
              |  G  >  C  > |G  >  D  > | G  >      C > |G  >   D > |
              |             |         I | love you, Lord, | and I lift my |
```

```
G >C > |G> G7 > |C  >G > |Am > G  > |D    >>    | D7  >
voice  |     To | worship | You, O my | soul  re joice. |
```

```
  >  | G  >   C  > |G> D  > |G >C  >  |G>
Take | joy, my King, |  in what You | hear,   >  |
```

```
G7
{May it  >    |C   >G    > |Am7 >D7 > |G > C > |G
{Let me be a | sweet, sweet | sound in Your | ear.
```

22

G7 is the new chord:

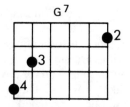

G^7

2. Pivot notes

G to G7 (3rd and 4th fingers)
Am7 to D7 (2nd finger)

3. Here is the 3rd song from list 2, *In My Life, Lord.*

```
1 2 3 4 | 1 2 3 4 | 1 2 3 4 | 1 2 3 4 | 1 2 3 4 |
        | C  G    | Am Em   | Dm G7   | C  G    | {C     (G) | Am    Em
        |         |         |         |         | {C ——————— | Em ———————
        |    >  > |   >  >  |   >  >  |   >  >  |    >   >   |   >     >
        |         |         |         |         | 1. In   my | life, Lord,
```

```
        { Dm ——————————— | B♭maj7 —— G7 |
        { Dm ——————————— | G7 ————————— |
        ( Dm —— G7 ——    | Dm ——————— G7 |
             >     >      |    >      >
          be glorified,  | be glorified.
```

```
{ C    (G) | Am   Em |          |        |
{ C ——————— | Em ———— | Dm    G7 |  C     |
     >   >  |   >   > |   >    >  |  >     |
  In my     | life, Lord, | be glorified to|day.
```

2. In my praise... 3. In this place....

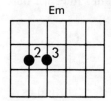

Em

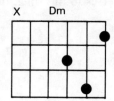

X   Dm

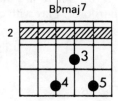

B♭maj7

4. Pivot notes

Am to Em (3rd finger)
Dm to G7 (2nd finger)

5. Bar chords

If you decide to use the chord of B♭maj7 in the first line, you'll need to place your index finger firmly on the fretboard, while at the same time checking to see that the strings aren't buzzing by strumming the strings very slowly.

When you've done that, place the other fingers into position and strum again, checking that no strings are buzzing.

This is a very difficult position to hold for any length of time at first, as the fingers and wrist are likely to ache. This is a natural reaction on the part of muscles that have not been stretched before, so don't worry. But you're going to have to master it some time, so why not start now?

It is worth considering that it will probably take you several months before you master the technique of the bar chord.

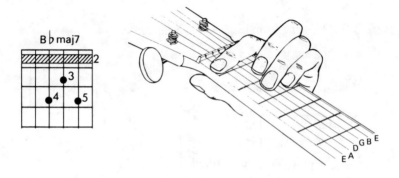

LESSON 8

1. Here is the first song from list 3 on page 47, *Bind Us Together (S.o.F. no. 6)*. There are more verses to this song, but one will suffice for our purposes. Play with capo 3.

```
1   2   3 | 1   2   3 | 1   2   3 | 1   2   3 | 1   2   3 | 1   2   3 |
                     D                          Em7         A7
          |         |>          |>          |>         |>         |
                                                                    D
                                                                    >
Chorus                                                              Bind us
```

```
      |>          |>         |>          Em7       A7
      to-gether, Lord, |  Bind us to-gether with | cords that | cannot be |
                                         >         >
```

```
D> |>        |>          |>         |>
bro-ken. | Bind us to-gether, Lord, | bind us to-gether, |
```

```
Em7         A7          D
>           >           > >  >
Bind us to| gether with | love. |
```

24

Verse 1

$$
\text{There is} \mid \overset{\text{G}}{\underset{>}{\text{only one}}} \mid \overset{\text{D}}{\underset{>}{\text{God,}}} \mid \; \overset{>}{} \mid
$$

$$
\left\{\begin{matrix}\text{Em}^7 \\ \text{D} >\end{matrix}\right. \quad \overset{\text{A7}}{\underset{>}{}} \qquad \overset{\text{D}}{\underset{>}{}}
$$
$$
\text{There is} \mid \text{only one} \mid \text{King,} \mid \; > \mid
$$

There is │ only one │ God, │ > │

{ Em⁷ / D > │ A7 > │ D > │ > │
There is │ only one │ King, │ > │

There is │ only one │ Body, │ > │

{ Em⁷ / D > │ A7 > │ D > │ > │
That is │ why we │ sing: │ > │

2. Here is the strumming.

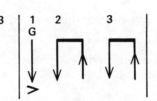

From looking at the diagram, you should be able to work out that

│ is equivalent to ⌐⌐ in duration.

3.

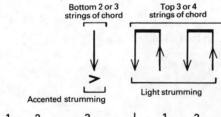

Bottom 2 or 3 strings of chord   Top 3 or 4 strings of chord

Accented strumming   Light strumming

4.

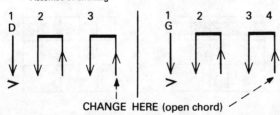

CHANGE HERE (open chord)

Also practise: Em7 to A7, A7 to D, D to G, and G to D.

5. Pivot notes

Em7 to A7 (3rd finger).

LESSON 9

1. Here is the 2nd song from list 3 on page 47, *Let There Be Love* (Capo 4) *(S.o.F. no. 80)*.

```
 1 2  3 4 5 6 | 1 2 3 4 5 6 | 1 2 3 4 5 6 | 1 2 3 4 5 6 | 1  2  3          |
              C                Dm            G7            C                |
              >        >       >       >     >       >     >        >       |
                                                                 Let there be
```

```
 Dm        >         G7                        C   (Em)    Am
 >         >         >        >                >      >    >
 love shared a-mong us, Let there be | love in our | eyes,
```

```
         >      Dm            G7
         >      >      >      >
 May now Your | love sweep this | nation,
```

```
              C      { C7
         >    >    > { A7
         >              >
 Cause us, O | Lord, to a-rise.
```

```
        { F
        { Dm            G7
  >       >      >      >
 Give us a | fresh under-standing
```

```
            C   >  (E7)    Am
     >      >       >      >
 Of brotherly | love that is | real,
```

```
            Dm            G7
     >      >      >      >
 Let there be | love shared a-mong us,
        { F——————— C
        { C -- Fmaj7 — C
     >         >
 Let there be | love.              |
```

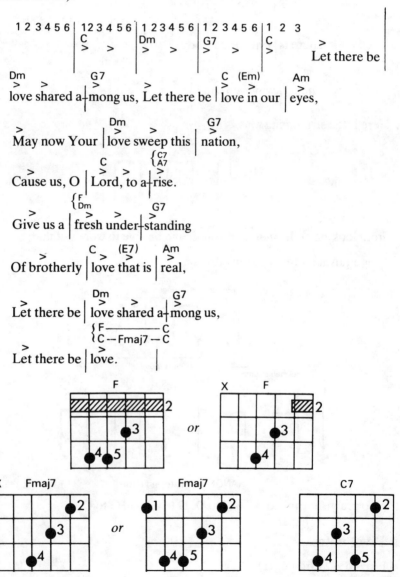

2. The F bar chord

The same applies to this chord as was said of the B♭maj chord in lesson 7, section 5. It isn't an easy chord to come to grips with. If you decide to use it, the chord before it should be C7. If you decide to use Dm instead of F, then use A7 instead of C7.

3. Pivot notes

Dm to G7 (2nd finger) Em to Am (3rd finger) C to Fmaj7 (2nd finger)
C to Em (3rd finger)   C to A7 (3rd finger)

4. *Worthy Art Thou (S.o.F. no. 157).*

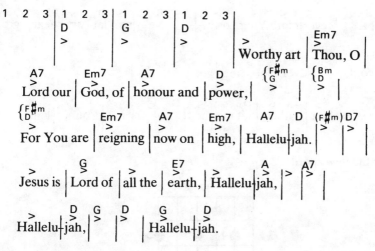

New chords (optional):

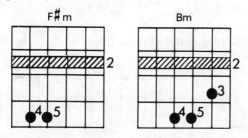

Note

If you decide to use the F♯m and Bm bar chords, refer back to lesson 7 section 5 for instructions.

LESSON 10

1. Here is the 4th strumming style in this series of lessons. The first song we're going to use to illustrate it with is from list 4 on page 48, *Abba Father* (Capo 3) (*S.o.F. no. 1*).

```
1   2   3 |1   2   3 |1   2   3 |1   2   3 |1   2   3 |           |           |
    G     |    D     |    C     |    G     |          |           |           |
        > > |      > > |      > > |      > > |   > >  |C> >     |D> >     |
          |          |          |          |   Abba  |Father,  |let me   |

  G   >> |C    >   > |D  >   > |G   >> |  >> |   >   > |C  >> |D  >   > |
   be    |Yours and |Yours a lone. |    |    |May my |will for |e—ver |

  G>  > |C>>  |D  >    > |G  >> | >> |B7  >    > |Em  >   > |B7   >    > |
   be   | ever more Your |own. |   |   |Ne—ver |let  my |heart  grow|

  Em    >  > |C   >   > |(Am)  >   > |D7  >   > | >   > |
   cold,    |Never |let   me |go.   |     |

  G    >   > |C>  >  |D>  >   > |G>> |C   >     >  |D  >   > |G  >
   A—bba |Father, |let me |be |You—rs and |Yours a lone.
                                                         |>
```

Note the new chord:

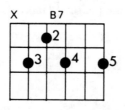

2. Here is the strumming pattern for the song:

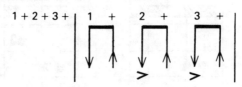

3.

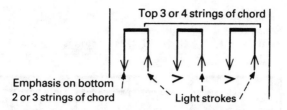

Top 3 or 4 strings of chord

Emphasis on bottom
2 or 3 strings of chord

Light strokes

Here is a graph to help you visualize the contrast in volume between each stroke:

4.

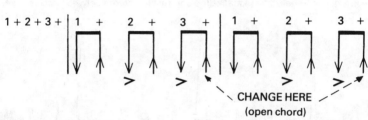

CHANGE HERE
(open chord)

Also practise C to D, D to G, G to B7, B7 to Em, Em to B7, Em to C, and C to D7.

5. Pivot notes

G to B7 (3rd finger)   C to Am (2nd and 3rd fingers)
B7 to Em (3rd finger)   C to D7 (2nd finger)

6. Here is an alternative strumming pattern for the song:

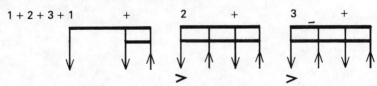

If you are at all confused by the above diagram, the following should help you.

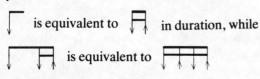 is equivalent to ⟍ in duration, while

⟍ is equivalent to ⟍

7.

Emphasis on bottom
2 or 3 strings of
chord

Top 3 or 4 strings of chord

1 + 2 + 3 +

Fairly
loud

Accents

Light strokes

Here is a graph to help you visualize the contrast in volume between each stroke.

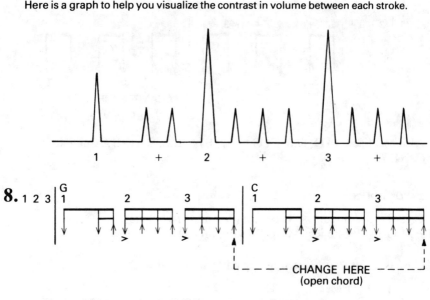

8. 1 2 3

G

C

CHANGE HERE
(open chord)

30

LESSON 11

1. Here is the 2nd song from list 4 on page 48, *For Unto Us a Child Is Born.*

```
1   2   3 | 1   2   3 | 1   2   3 | 1   2   3 | 1   2   3
          | G         | C         | G         | D
          |     >   > |     >   > |     >   > |    >    >     G>>
          |          |          |          |         For unto | us a |
```

```
(G7)    >   > | C >> | Am >>      | D  >  > | son  >   > | G  >  >
   chi—ld is  | born, |      Unto | us   a |          is | given, |
```

```
(G7) >  >       | C    >   >  |       >   > | G >  >
     And the    | go—vern+ment shall | be upon His | shoulder,      >
```

```
       >        | D   >   > | C        >
   And His      | name shall be | called  >
```

```
       >        | G  >   > | D7 >       > | G >> | G7
   Wonder+ful Counsel+lor, the Mighty | God,    |  >
```

```
   >   | C >> |     >   > | G  >  > |
   The | Ever+lasting | Fa——| ther,  >
```

```
       >        | D   >   > |     >  > | G
   And the      | Prince of | Peace is | He.  >
                                         >
```

2. The strumming patterns in lesson 10 can be used for all the songs in list 4 on page 48, though some of the songs might be better played with this alternative strumming:

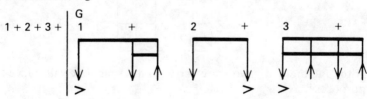

3.

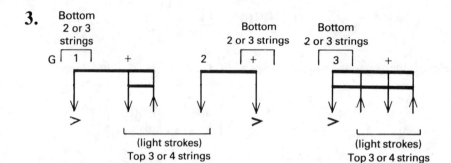

4. Here is the 3rd song from list 4,
River Wash Over Me (Capo 3) (*S.o.F. no. 107*).

```
1   2   3 |1   2   3 |1   2   3 |1   2   3 |1   2   3 |
          C           Dm          C           G           C  >  >  G    >  >
              >   >         >   >      >   >      >   >    River| wash over
```

```
Am    >   >  |   > > | Dm       >   > | G7  >  > | Em  > > |   > > |
me,                    Cleanse me and | make me  | new.
```

```
{ F
{ Dm      >  >  | G7    >     >  | C    >  > | Am  >  > |
Bathe me, re-fresh me and | fill me a-new,
```

```
Dm    >   >  | C/G   G  | C   |
             |  >    >  | >   |
River wash   | o—ver    | me.
```

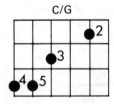

C/G

Although there are two more verses to this song, one will suffice for our
purposes here.

5. Pivot notes

Dm to G7 (2nd finger)
C to Am (2nd and 3rd fingers)

LESSON 12

1. Here is the first song from list 5 on page 48, *Praise Him*.

```
1   2   3   4 | 1   2   3   4 | 1   2   3   4 |
              |   G  >  C  >  |   G  >  D  >  | G  >        >  | G7 >        >
                                         1.| Praise Him,   | praise Him,
```

C   >   >
Praise Him in the morning, |

      >   G   >
Praise Him in the noontime. |

    >   > | B7 >   Em > |
Praise Him, | praise Him, |

Am7   >   D7 > | G
Praise Him when the sun goes | down.
                                       >

2. Love Him . . .   3. Trust Him . . .   4. Serve Him . . .

2. Here is the strumming:

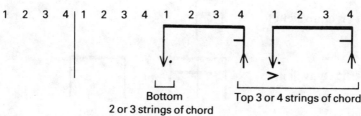

```
1   2   3   4 | 1   2   3   4    1   2   3   4    1   2   3   4
```

Bottom
2 or 3 strings of chord

Top 3 or 4 strings of chord

3. (a)

```
1   2   3   4   1   2   3   4    1   2   3   4  →  G C G D
```

G

>

(b)

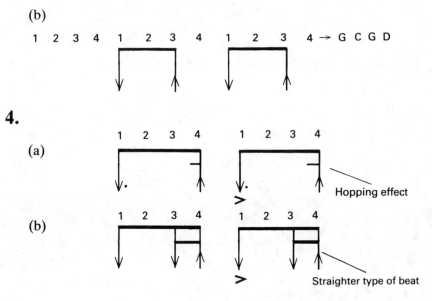

1 2 3 4   1   2   3   4   1   2   3   4 → G C G D

4.

(a)

1 2 3 4   1 2 3 4

Hopping effect

(b)

1 2 3 4   1 2 3 4

Straighter type of beat

5. If the above is difficult to understand, the following should clarify the situation.

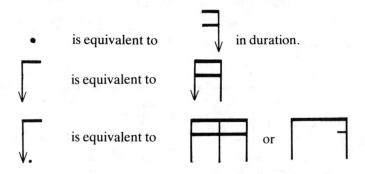

• is equivalent to ☐ in duration.

☐ is equivalent to ☐

☐ is equivalent to ☐ or ☐

6. Pivot notes

G to G7 (3rd and 4th fingers)
G to B7 (3rd finger)
B7 to Em (3rd finger)
Am7 to D7 (2nd finger)

LESSON 13

1. Here is the second song from list 5 on page 48, *Our God Reigns* (Capo 2) *(S.o.F. no. 41)*.

```
1   2   3   4 │1   2   3   4│1   2   3   4│1   2   3   4│
              G    .    >    >│D    >    >│C    >    >│  G              >   >
                                                          How lovely

        C  > .> │D    >         >│G  >     >
        on   the │mountains are the │feet of Him │

       (Em) >         > │Am >  >D>     >│G   >   >
        Who brings good │news,    │  good │news,    │

       (G7) >       > C  >  >│D   >        > │G  >      >│(Em) >
        Proclaiming │ peace, announcing news of │ happiness.

              >  │Am  >  >│D >      >│G      >(C) >│(G7) >
        Our God │reigns,  │ Our God │reigns. >  │

              >  │C  >  >│ >     >│G  > >.    >
        Our God │reigns,  │ Our God │reigns, ├───

              >  │C>  >│D>     >│G    >(C)   G
        Our God │reigns,├── Our God │reigns. >  │ >
```

2. Here is the 3rd song from list 5, *How Great Is Our God* (Capo 3) *(S.o.F. no. 39)*.

```
1  2  3  4│1 2 3 4│1 2 3 4│1 2 3 4│1  2
          D   >   >│A   >   >│G   >   >│D   >          > (Em7)  > >
                                         How great is our │ God,    │

       A7  >         > │D  > (G)> │D
        How great is His │ name,    │

          >         > │(Em7)>   > │A7  >        > │D  >(G)>│D
        How great is His │ love,    │ For ever the │ same. │

          >         >   │ >    >│(D7) >                 > │G   >   >
        He rolled back the │ wa—ters │ of the mighty Red │ Sea,   │

      {Em7
      {E7  >    (A7)        >  │D  >   >│{Em7       A7  > │D  >(G)>│D
      {E7>                                                          >
        And He said, I'll never │ leave you, │ Put your trust in │ Me.
```

35

Note alternative finger
positions, which may be
easier on some occasions.

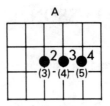

A

LESSON 14

1. *Within the Veil (S.o.F. no. 155.)*

```
1   2   3   4 | 1   2   3   4 | 1   2   3   4 | 1   2 · 3   4 |
              |  C            |  Dm           |  G7           |
              |  >   > >   >  |  >   > >   >  |  >   > >   >  |

1   2       3   4
C                       | Dm          |  G7
>           > >   >  |  >  > >   >  | >   > >           >  |
       With — in the |  veil           |  I now would      |
```

```
Cmaj7           (Am7)                  Dm                    G7                    Cmaj7
  >   > >   >  | >   > >       >  | >   >   >   >  | >   >   >       >  | >   >   >   >  |
come,            | In — to the   |  Holy Place    |  To look up —  |  on Thy face.  |
```

```
(A7)                          Dm                     G7                    (Cmaj7)
  >   >   >       >  | >   >   >       >  | >   > >       >  | >   >   >   >  |
  I   see such   |  beauty there,  |  No other       |  can compare,  |
```

```
(A7)                          Dm                            G7                    C   (Fmaj7)  C
  >   >   >       >  | >   >   >       >  | >   >   >       >  | >   >   > > | >  |
  I   worship    |  Thee, my Lord, |  With — in the |  veil.           |
```

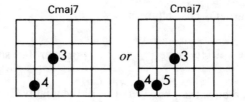

Cmaj7   or   Cmaj7

36

2. Here is the strumming pattern:

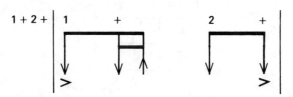

3.

Bottom 2 or 3 strings of chord | Top 3 or 4 strings of chord | Bottom 2 or 3 strings of chord

4. Pivot notes

Dm to G7 (1st finger) Cmaj7 to A7 (3rd finger)
Cmaj7 to Am7 (3rd finger)

5. *Hallelujah, My Father* (Capo 2.)

```
1   2   3   4 | 1   2   3   4 | 1   2   3   4 | 1   2   3   4 | 1 2 3
              D                 A                 G                 D
              >       > >   >   >       > >   >   >       > >   >   > > >
```

```
    4     A                       A                   G
    >     >       >   >   >       >   >     >     >   >       > >   >
Halle lu——jah,  my | Fa——ther, for | giving us Your |
```

```
D
>     > >   >     |   >       >   > >|>       >       >       >
Son,              | Sending Him  in to the world   to be |
```

```
G                     D               G                      {F♯m
>       >   >     >   >   > >   >     >           > >        {D    >   >   >
given up  for     | men,            | Knowing  we would | bruise Him   And |
```

```
    G     (D)   E7        {A7 sus 4 – A7        D                 A
    >     >     >     >   {A7   > >     >     > >       >     > >|>  >   >     >
smite Him from the | earth.——  Halle lu——jah, my | Father, in His |
```

```
G               D             A               G             D
>     > >   >   >   >   >     >|>   >   >   >   >   > >   >   >   > >   >|>
death is my | birth.   Ha-lle lu jah,  my | Father, in His | life is my | life.
```

37

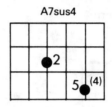

A7sus4

Note

(a) If you decide to use the F♯m bar chord instead of D, refer back to lesson 7 section 5 for instructions.

(b) The D chord used throughout this song uses all 6 strings. I prefer it to the normal D chord because it produces a much fuller sound. I refer to it as D/F♯.

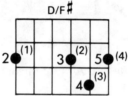

D/F♯

6. *He Is Lord (S.o.F. no. 31).*

```
1  2  3  4 |1  2  3  4 |1  2  3  4 |1  2  3  4  |
            G           C           G           Am7        D7
            >     > > > |>     > > > |>  > > >  |>  > > > |>>> >  >|
                                     1. He is | Lord,  |  He is |

G    (C)  G          Em            {Bm         Am7        D
>  > >> > |> > >  > |>  >>     >  {A7  >  >  > |>> >> |> >
Lord,     |    He is | risen from the| dead and He is | Lord. |

            G          G7          C          Am7
>     >  |> > >  > |> >> > |> >>> > |> 
Every |knee shall| bow, every |tongue con-fess

(D7)      G   (Em)  (Cmaj7) D7  C          G
>   >  |> >> >  >|> >> >>> > |> 
That | Je—sus | Christ is | Lord.
```

2. He's my Lord . . .
3. You're my Lord . . .
4. You're our Lord . . .

LESSON 15

1. Let's look at the 7th type of strumming. Here is the first song from list 7 on page 48, *Unto Thee, O Lord*.

1 2 3 4 | 1 2 3 4 | 1 2 3 4 | 1 2 3 4 |

G
>   > | D   >   > | C   >   > | G

Únto Thee, Ó|

Lord, (Únto Thee, Ó | Lord,) Dŏ I lift up̆ my |

D   >
soul, (Dŏ I lift up̆ my | soul,) Únto Thee, Ó | Lord, (Únto Thee, Ó |

Lord,) Dŏ I lift up̆ my | G soul, (Dŏ I lift up̆ my | soul,) >

O my̆ | God, (O my̆ | G7 God,) >

I trust in | C Thee, (I trust in | Thee,) >

(Am7) >   (D7)   > | G
Let me not be a|shamed,

        (Em)   (Am7) D7   G (C)   G
Let not my enemies | triumph over | me. | >

2. Here is the strumming:

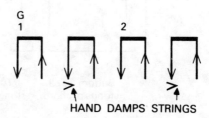

HAND DAMPS STRINGS

39

3. Damping

(a) This is done by momentarily stopping the strings from vibrating *after* the 2nd stroke and *on* the 3rd (see section 2 above).

(b) The length of the arc of the stroke responsible for the damping remains the same as the other strokes.

(c) Even more 'bite' can be produced if you strum further up the strings than usual, on the section of the fretboard beside the sound hole.

(d) The side of the hand from the wrist to half way up the little finger is used for damping.

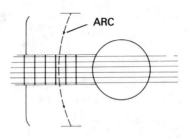

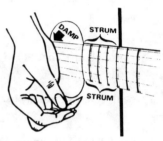

4.

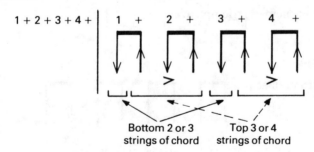

5. Here is an alternative strumming pattern with the damping action omitted.

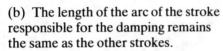

40

LESSON 16

1. Here is the 2nd song from list 7, *Where the Spirit of the Lord Is* (Capo 1).

```
1  2  3  4 │1  2  3  4 │1  2  3  4 │1  2  3  4 │1  2      3      4  │  ╲
           │ G         │ C         │ D         │ G                  │
           │    >   >  │    >   >  │    >   >  │    >            >  │
           │           │           │           │       Where the   │
```
                                                                        repeat

```
     >           >  │ >         >  │        >        >  │
Spirit of the Lord is, │  Where the │ Spirit of the Lord is, │
```

```
G7 >          >  C  >         >  │ >        >  G >     >  │
      There is │ li —berty, │      there is │ liberty. │
```

```
  >     >  │ D        >        >  │
And I will │ praise You, O Lord, │
```

```
  >     >  │ G        >        >  │
And I will │ praise You, O Lord, │
```
                                                        repeat

```
  >     >  │ D        >        >  │ >
And I will │ praise You, O Lord, │
```

```
          C  G    C  G  │
  >       >  >    >  >   │
In the │ Spirit.          │
```

STRUMMING PATTERNS

KEY

⌐____⌐ Play the bottom 2 or 3 strings of the chord.
⌐----⌐ Play the top 3 or 4 strings of the chord.

CHORD CHART

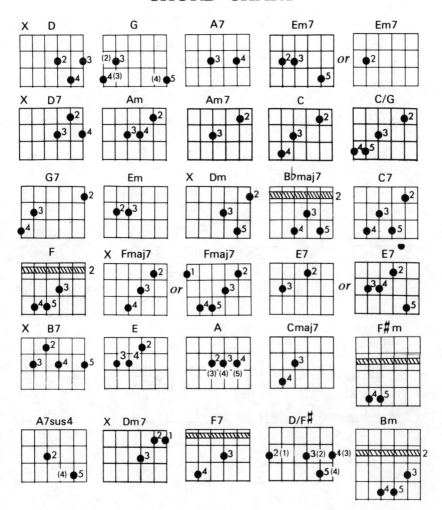

KEY

X   Don't play that string.

    Bar chord— see lesson 7 section 5 and also page 45.

Numbers in brackets indicate alternative fingerings.

ADDITIONAL CHORDS

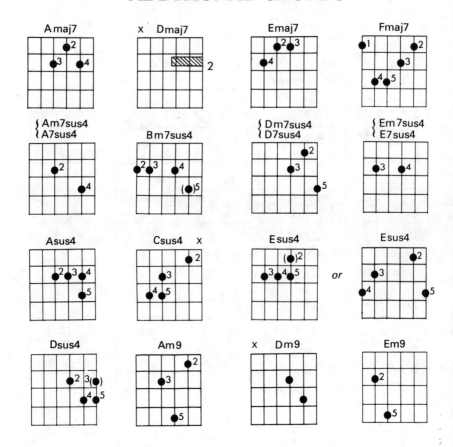

44

THE USE OF THE BAR CHORD

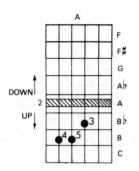

To find B♭, B.C and so on, simply move this position *up* ↓ the fingerboard. Similarly, to find A♭, G, F♯ and F, move this position ↑ *down* the fingerboard.

This technique can be applied to all the other chords listed below when trying to find chords of a similar nature, i.e. A7 to B♭7 to B7 ↓ and A7 to A♭7 to G7 ↑ Am to B♭m to Bm ↓ and Am to B♭m to Bm ↑ and so on.

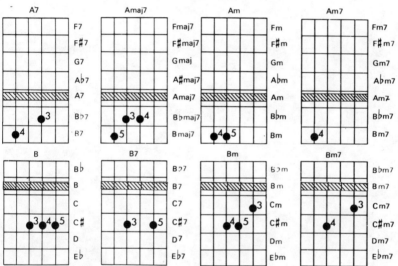

The use of the half-bar
Take note of what strings are *not* to be played.

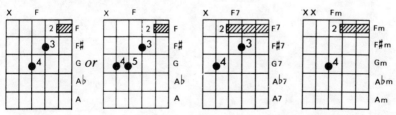

This same technique of moving the shape of a chord up and down the fingerboard to find chords of a similar nature can also be applied to the following:

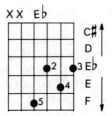 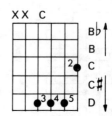

STRUMMING GROUPS

(*Songs of Fellowship* numbers are in brackets.)

List 1
I Will Enter His Gates (62)
For I'm Building a People of Power (25)
Hallelujah, for the Lord Our God... (30)
Make a Joyful Noise (90)
My Heart Overflows (91)
For as Truly as I Live (24)
Lift Jesus Higher (82)
O Give Thanks (97)
Rejoice in the Lord Always (106)
Break Forth into Joy (9)
I Will Extol You (63)
This Is the Day (130)

List 2
We Are More Than Conquerors
I Love You, Lord (49)
In My Life, Lord
Jesus, How Lovely You Are (68)
Jesus, Take Me As I Am (75)
Jesus (Your Love) (72)
When I Feel the Touch (153)
Lord God, Heavenly King (83)
You Are the King of Glory (158)

List 3
Bind Us Together (6)
Let There Be Love (80)
Worthy Art Thou (157)
Jesus, Name Above All Names (73)
I Will Sing Unto the Lord (66)
Love One Another (89)
My Peace (95)
We Worship Thee (152)
Sing Unto God (111)

List 4

Abba Father (1)
For Unto Us a Child Is Born
River Wash Over Me (107)
I Receive Your Love (53)
Set My Spirit Free (109)
Jesus I Come (69)
Jesus Is Lord (71)

List 5

Praise Him, Praise Him
Our God Reigns (41)
How Great Is Our God (39)
Therefore the Redeemed (127)
The Nations Shall See You Justified (125)
O Lord, You've Done Great Things (100)
Come Bless the Lord (16)
Thy Loving Kindness (133)
City, O City (12)

List 6

Within the Veil (155)
Hallelujah, My Father
He Is Lord (36)
We Have Come Into This Place (146)
Come and Praise Him, Royal Priesthood (14)
O Father, I Do Love You (96)
Father, We Love You (22)
Jesus, Stand Among Us (74)
Do Not Strive (79)
For We See Jesus (26)
His Name Is Higher (37)
I Stand Before the Presence (55)
I Hear the Sound of Rustling (48)

List 7

Unto Thee, O Lord
Where the Spirit of the Lord Is
I'm Forgiven (44)
Break Forth and Sing for Joy (8)
Sing Unto the Lord a New Song (112)
We'll Sing a New Song (147)

Part Two

Leading Worship

1

SOME PRACTICAL HINTS

In any meeting, people need to feel at ease with the person who is leading them. You have to grant them a sense of security and you can do this by making due preparation beforehand, spending time in prayer and practice. If you are going to be using new songs in your time of worship, it might be helpful to teach them to people at the beginning of the meeting and only later to use them in worship. People often find it difficult to put their hearts into a new song before they feel confident with the words and tune.

When you come to the meeting, remember you have come to *minister*. Don't just play your instrument because the singing sounds rather hollow without an accompaniment, or because your guitar has been gathering for too long the dust of neglect in the attic. Ask God to anoint what you do, with the aim of giving him pleasure, showing appreciation and gratitude to him, and building each other up. Psalm 104:1 says, 'Bless the Lord, O my soul,' so the Lord can be blessed, moved by our heartfelt praise.

You must also realize that it isn't *just* you or *just* the Holy Spirit who is ministering, but that you're doing it together—firstly to God and secondly to people.

Introduce the fact that you are about to worship. In some Christian circles, when people come to a time of singing, there is a tendency to use the songs we've been looking at in this book to have a 'sing-song'. The outcome can sometimes be a kind of 'Bingo-worship' whereby various people at random shout out the number of their favourite song. This will not help people sense God's presence or cause them to expect him to touch them in worship.

Psalm 68:4 exhorts us to 'sing praises' to the Lord. The verse talks of praises, not songs. It is possible to sing songs and not to praise. We only praise when we have placed ourselves in contact with the Lord and are addressing our songs to him with our hearts.

Try to prepare people for getting into an attitude of worship by telling them to stand (Ps 134:1; 135:2). There will be a vast difference in the quality and volume of singing when a group of people stand, compared to when they are seated.

Ask them to close their eyes and to be quiet and still. This will help them force out external distractions, such as the dandruff on the head in front, and focus in on God.

You may wish to briefly introduce the first song in such a way as to inspire thoughtful worship. (See *Hindrances to Praise* below.) Then introduce the song musically. Make sure this is *well rehearsed*. If you start playing timidly, the chances are the singing will also be timid. Therefore, accent the strumming clearly in your brief musical introduction, so that you can create a regular pulse, preparing people to sing in time.

As you play these few bars of well-rehearsed introduction, you will probably be the only one who knows where the vocal melody comes in, so start singing the first line of the song, giving a clear melodic lead line. As you do, the others will join in. Again, if you enter timidly, this will transmit itself to the others, so *practise this thoroughly on your own* until you are confident you will be able to do it decisively in public.

You may think you can't combine playing and singing, especially with having to maintain these regular accents on the guitar. If you feel it will be too much to cope with for a whole song, at least practise combining the first line of the song with the guitar accompaniment. People, in the main, will be looking to you to give them the lead into the song. You must be prepared to grant them this. After that, your own singing contribution can probably diminish if need be.

Maintain strong accents on the guitar throughout. This will insure against people who have a tendency to stray behind the beat when singing, which can create chaos if they also happen to be equipped with a loud voice!

Should you sense at any time that people need further encouragement to worship, it might be helpful to gently bring the singing to a halt after having sung a song through a few times, and briefly say something to the effect that the Holy Spirit wants to minister the words of the songs you've been singing to each person present.

For example, in the song *In My Life, Lord,* you can change that line each time to 'In my praise', 'In my prayers', 'In my work', 'In my home',

'In my street', or 'In our praise' etc. Then, you could drop the volume of the guitar playing and make the worship much more meditative, as you sing 'In my thoughts', 'On my lips', and then raise the volume of your playing, preparing people to sing 'In my life' for the last time in triumphant fashion.

There may be times when you're praying about a person or a couple who are weighed down by problems and generally going under the pressures of life. You could, if you felt it was right, allow the Holy Spirit to minister to them, as you sing the song *River Wash Over Me,* inserting the word 'him', 'her', 'them' or even the person's name, as you do so. You could also use this technique when praying about places: 'River, wash over (*name of place*)', though admittedly it might be difficult to fit Chipping Norton into the metre of the song!

Try developing the theme of a song so that, by the second or third time of singing it, the sentiment of the words has not been lost. For example, in singing the song *He Is Lord,* on the repeat, sing, 'You're our Lord', and then 'He's my Lord'. Then, bring the volume of your guitar playing down so that you prepare people for a change. As you do so, say, 'Let's sing, "You're My Lord", softly.' Maybe as you come to the end of that verse, get people to sing it even more softly, prayerfully. As they come to the end of that verse, you could start to play more loudly and say, 'He is Lord, last time', which you could do in celebratory style. If you don't wish to say 'last time', remember to steer the singing at the very end by playing more slowly with a sense of climax, so that people are in no doubt that they've now finished with that particular song.

Use the songs you learn in your prayer meetings to underline and punctuate your prayers, so that you give them an extra meaning and dimension. It doesn't have to be all singing followed by all praying, finished off with all singing again. This way your singing will *become* a part of your praying, and both are integrated into a time of complete worship.

Avoid the predictable treatment of songs. Without variation there is always the danger of ending up in a sort of mindless repetition. A very common technique which can bring a breath of fresh air to the singing of a song, is to allow people to sing it through once, then to hand it first to the ladies, then to the men, and finally to sing it through together. Or if a song divides up quite happily into two sections, apply the same technique there.

Although it is important to have a steady, fresh input of new songs and techniques designed to help us worship, the real issue is in fact whether or not people *really want to worship*. If people's lives are not totally surrendered to Christ, such efforts to aid them in praise will only be misleading and frustrating.

As you play, try to create areas of light and shade (dynamics). Vary the volume of different verses—although not so much so that people become confused. You could have one verse sung very quietly and another hummed. With all of these, you'll need to indicate what is to happen in the next verse by saying a few words of direction in the gap between verses, dropping the volume of your guitar playing slightly so that people can hear your instructions. Again, this is something you need to practise away from the meeting.

Another technique you might try is to prepare a short, appropriate passage of Scripture and get someone to read this out over a verse or two of a song where you've indicated to people that you're going to hum softly while listening to the reading.

Try to have a block time of worship sometimes, where people can sense God's presence. Avoid unnecessary breaks. It might help you if you were to have a list of songs in front of you so that at a glance you're able to see a song which could go straight on, thematically, from the one you've just sung. For example, *Jesus, Name Above All Names* can be used quite happily in conjunction with *Open Our Eyes, Lord*. You could lead people to sing *Jesus, Name Above All Names* a few times, then without any break, sing, *Open Our Eyes, Lord*, maybe humming that through the second time, finally coming back to sing *Jesus, Name Above All Names*.

You could get together a file of songs, one song to a page in alphabetical order, so that as your repertoire expands, you can insert each song without disrupting the order. The loose-leaf edition of *Songs of Fellowship* is tailor-made for this purpose. If you're using songs written out by yourself, make sure as you write the words out that you leave a space above them for the chords. (Don't forget that you will need to clear copyright if you copy someone else's song.) At the front of the file, make a list of these songs in alphabetical order, so that without much head-scratching you're able to bring songs in that are going to help people keep their minds focused on God in praise.

You could even have a list of the strumming patterns on one page at the front, numbered 1 to 7. Then at the top right-hand corner of each song page you can write the number of the strumming pattern, together with the capo number.

You might also draw up two lists, one containing the more joyful, up-tempo songs and another containing the quieter, slower songs; or lists of songs that link together thematically. Whatever method you employ, try to prepare yourself so that you're never at a loss over what to play next.

Before you launch into playing, check that you're in the right key, or else you could have a few casualties on your hands, with people either leaping for notes which are so high that only dogs can hear them, or grovelling around in the depths.

Be prepared to help the praise take off by practising possible key changes. Make these changes definite so that people are not left singing in the old key while you have moved on to the new key. You'll momentarily have to raise the volume of your playing as you make the change of key between verses, so that people are left in no doubt as to what is happening.

Music isn't the be-all-and-end-all of the meeting, so try and be sensitive to what else is going on. As you lead, keep in mind how long people have been sitting or standing. If they've been standing through a few songs you may feel it right to tell them to sit down. But do so in such a way that the worship is not interrupted.

Try not to project your feelings onto the meeting. Leave whatever happens with the Lord, asking him to wipe away anything which was from you and to sustain that which was from him. It isn't up to you to gauge how many people were touched by God during the meeting. If you get onto this wrong train of thought, the meeting will only be as good as *you* felt throughout it. So try not to be subjective.

There will be different people of different temperaments and moods present. Some may be feeling full of get-up-and-go, whereas others may be feeling that all their get-up-and-go has got up and gone. Some may be enjoying spiritual mountain-top experiences, whereas others may be quietly backsliding. Some may be recommitting their lives to God, while others may have just committed their lives to him for the first time. Therefore you may wish to contrast the use of joyful up-tempo songs with the more meditative ones, always being sensitive to the Spirit's leading. Times of jubilation can be contrasted with times of silence.

In silence, there is little opportunity for our egos to cover up the emptiness. Often in noise and activity, the ego can protect itself by projecting itself. Don't be afraid of silence; stability is to be found in the balance of contemplation and action.

God wants to trust us with silence, and we must be willing to wait and give him our attention and hear what he has to say. So often we barge into his presence and assert ourselves on him with an endless parade of prayers and songs, and then we barge out again.

Psalm 68:32–33 says, 'Sing to God...sing praises to the Lord...who thunders with a mighty voice.' So communication with God through praise is a two-way street. Like communicating by telephone, we can't see the person on the other end of the line, but our part in the conversation consists of words and silences.

It is clear from the Bible that some men saw a place for music in prophecy—i.e. to bring the mind of God into a particular situation. One such person was Elisha. In 2 Kings 3:11–19, King Jehoshaphat is needing advice from God, so he calls for God's man of the moment, Elisha. Elisha doesn't tell him to organize a prayer meeting. Instead, he simply calls for a musician who begins to play his instrument. As the musician strums, God speaks through Elisha and the King receives his directions.

This isn't something just for Old Testament times; it is a principle that God wants us to understand and apply *now* in our own situations. He may want to speak, or he may not. But the question is: are we willing to allow him to?

Help people to understand that praise should be governed by the will, because sometimes we simply don't feel like communicating with God in prayer, let alone singing. When negative feelings clamour for a hearing, it is important to understand the concept of 'a sacrifice of praise'. The Scriptures exhort us to '*continually* offer to God a *sacrifice* of praise' (Heb 13:15). This is a command of love and, as with all God's commands, a prescription for our well-being. He will honour our obedience.

A story which underlines the truth of this spiritual principle is told by Richard Wurmbrand who was held prisoner in a communist prison for fourteen years on account of his Christian faith. At one time he was put on a ration of bread and water. When the guard brought the food in, he looked at it vacantly, and tried desperately to give thanks and praise to God, for he remembered the scripture: '*Rejoice* when you are accused falsely and treated unrighteously for my sake....'

So he gave thanks and tried to rejoice and give thanks for the food, at which point he remembered that the verse went on to say, '...and leap for joy...'! He had never done this before, but he reluctantly got to his feet and started to dance round the food.

The guard, wondering what was going on in the cell, peered through the shutter in the door and, thinking the prisoner to have had a brainstorm, sent word back to his superiors informing them of the situation.

They can't have liked the idea of their prisoners having brainstorms, because they decided to remedy the situation by ordering the guard to give him a decent, nourishing meal.

As the guard opened the cell door and brought in the food, Richard Wurmbrand remembered the rest of the verse: '...*and great shall be your reward*'!

Another great example of sacrificial praise having repercussions in the spiritual domain is in Acts 16 where Paul and Silas are in prison. They have been stripped, severely flogged and put in chains, and yet we find them in verse 25 praying and singing to God at midnight (quite an uncommon occurrence in most prisons, I would imagine). God has promised in Psalm 22:3 that he will 'inhabit the praises of his people'. In this case, the result was a premature release from imprisonment, as the jail simply fell down. A dynamite prayer meeting, you could say.

We will be as rich as our relationship with God. Everything depends on that. Although it will be extremely difficult at times, we must try not to allow ourselves to wallow in our feelings and cut the lines of communication with God.

A brief word about the need for praise sometimes to be a sacrifice might help some people who are going through a hard time at home, at work or in a relationship. It might stop them falling into the trap of thinking that they can only praise when they feel like it.

Jonah 2:9 says, 'I will sacrifice to you with a voice of thanksgiving.' Jonah at this time was speaking to God from inside a large fish. He had a choice in his captivity: either to allow his fear to rule him, or to rule the fear with sacrificial praise. To allow the atmosphere to transform him, or to transform the atmosphere with sacrificial praise.

Psalm 81 talks about this sort of praise. Here, God simply says to his people, 'Open your mouth wide and I will fill it.' God is saying, if you feel you just can't praise because your whole being seems to be monopolized by negative feelings, he will nevertheless give you that praise if first you do your part and open your mouth. Psalm 81:11 sadly tells us, 'But my people would not listen to my voice, and Israel would have none of me.' Encourage people not to shut out God's voice and turn away from his presence, but to keep the lines of communication open, no matter how they are feeling.

2

HINDRANCES TO PRAISE

Satanic interference

Worship is the oxygen of heaven. It is at the centre of God's thinking. He wants a worshipping people.

Satan hates worship because it is so close to God's heart. He hates to see his enemy adored, and he knows there is power in praise. We see that exemplified in the incident with Paul and Silas (Acts 16:25–26). If prayer is like a gun, praise is like a tank.

The apostle Paul tells us: 'The god of this age has blinded the minds of unbelievers, so that they cannot see the light of the gospel of the glory of Christ' (2 Cor 4:4). So how do we take off the spiritual blindfolds which shroud people's minds in darkness? In 2 Corinthians 10:4 he says, 'The weapons we fight with are not the weapons of the world.' We wage war against spiritual forces, and when we are praying about situations, we need to look and see who really is at work there. As we place our spiritual music into God's hands, he will use it to tear down Satan's strongholds in people and situations.

A good example of this can be found in 1 Samuel 16:14–17, 23. Saul was being troubled by an evil spirit. Whenever it came to him, he became downcast. No one prayed for deliverance, no one laid hands on him, he didn't fast; he simply called for David to play his harp. A strange thing to do, you might think. But as soon as he played, the evil spirit left Saul. This is a spiritual principle that God wants us to recognize and use as a practical element in releasing people from spiritual bondage, so that they can become free moral agents, ready to exercise that free will for or against Christ.

It is often in times of worship that spiritual eyes are opened and people are won for Christ. Jesus made it clear that unless we first bind the strong man we will be unsuccessful in taking his property (Mk 3:27). Psalm

149:6–9 points out that 'with the *high praises* of God in their mouths, they bind their kings with chains and their nobles with fetters of iron'. This passage can now be taken to refer to the kings and nobles of the spiritual world which Paul talked about when listing Satan's power structure in Ephesians 6:12. Since we do battle against spiritual forces, we need spiritual weapons. But we also need to learn how and when to use them.

In 2 Chronicles 20 King Jehoshaphat and his kingdom of Judah were surrounded by powerful enemies who were about to invade them. Jehoshaphat didn't have sufficient military weaponry to pose a threat to the opposition, so he wisely turned to God for help (v. 12).

It was admitting his helplessness before God that enabled the Lord to go into action: 'The battle is not yours, but God's' (v. 15). Yet they still had a part to play: 'You will not have to fight this battle. Take up your positions...' (v. 17). Verse 21 describes what that position was. He 'appointed men to sing to the Lord and to praise him for the splendour of his holiness as they went out at *the head* of the army.' This simply shows us that praise came first in the proceedings. Verse 22 goes on to tell us the result of this praise: 'As they began to sing and praise, the Lord set ambushes against the men...who were invading Judah, and they were defeated.'

As with Jehoshaphat, there will be circumstances from time to time which we just will not be able to deal with ourselves, times when we will have to admit our inadequacy. God may allow them in order to teach us that certain situations can only be dealt with by employing the secret weapon of praise.

'Submit yourselves to God. Resist the devil, and he will flee from you' (Jas 4:7).

Fear

Our concepts of praise often vary according to our own personalities and backgrounds, so to get a true perspective on the matter, we need to go to the Bible.

In addition to the twenty references regarding the playing of musical instruments, and over 350 to singing (pitch never being mentioned, just a joyful *noise*), there are many references exhorting us to express our praise using the whole of our beings—mind, body and spirit.

Here are some of them: clapping (Ps 47:1; also used figuratively of the creation—Ps 98:8; Is 55:12); musical (especially stringed) instruments (Ps 33:2; 57:8; 144:9; 147:7; 149:3; 150:3–5); dancing (2 Sam 6:14; Ps 30:11; 149:3; 150:4); leaping (2 Sam 6:16; Acts 3:8); bowing and kneeling

(Ps 95:6; Eph 3:14); raising hands (Ps 63:4; 134:2; 141:2; Lam 3:41).

If this was how people used to worship in Old Testament times, then how much more should we with the New Testament be able to express ourselves to God. Is it simply that we British aren't a demonstrative sort of people when it comes to an outward show of feelings and emotions, or are there other reasons?

One of Satan's chief aims is to immobilize God's people, and one of his main devices for rendering us ineffective is fear—fear of the future, people, rejection, the dark, death, God...whatever is likely to bring a shadow of discord down on our lives.

In the area of praise he remains active, trying to wrap us up in being afraid of what others would think if we were to pray out loud or raise our hands in the air. We have seen that King Jehoshaphat's secret was to keep his eyes on God. This must be our secret too. And as we get to know, accept and love each other, our fears of how we express ourselves in worship will evaporate. We must cease being suspicious of one another. If we look for reasons to criticize the way someone worships, we'll find them. Let's accept one another whether we worship God with our hands in our pockets or in the air.

Having said that, I do recognize that many people find great difficulty with this whole area of raising hands in worship, and that whenever they have been encouraged to express themselves in such a way, they have been overcome with a sudden plague of arm paralysis.

It is quite understandable for people to feel inhibited, uncomfortable and self-conscious. But we need to understand that it is not a mindless, unthinking, present-day phenomenon but a Bible-based gesture of inner surrender and acclamation.

If someone walked up to the cashier's desk at a bank with a loaded pistol and told them, 'This is a hold up!' the cashier's hands would go up as a sign of surrender. At a football match when a goal is scored, up go the hands as a sign of acclamation. Similarly in our praise, this practice should convey either or both of these sentiments.

However we express ourselves in worship, let's recognize that we are part of the family of God. Like the members of any family, we all have our different habits, mannerisms and idiosyncrasies, but the only way to stay in tune with each other is to accept one another *just as we are*.

God hasn't given us a spirit of fear. 'Where the Spirit of the Lord is, there is freedom' (2 Cor 3:17).

Sin

Worship is not the occupation of a building for one fugitive hour a week. It is a way of life, dedicated to pleasing God, and is expressed in a concern for others (see Rom 12:1).

Essentially, worship stems out of the relationship between God and his people. When this relationship is broken through sin or unforgiveness, a barrier is created between us and all that he has for us through his Holy Spirit. 'Your iniquities have separated you from your God; your sins have hidden his face from you, so that he will not hear' (Is 59:2).

While sin sits undisturbed in our souls, our worship is superficial and deceptive. But as we come into the heat of God's presence, those wrong thoughts, words and actions which we have turned a blind eye to and forced down into our subconscious will begin to surface.

This is especially true in the area of unforgiveness. We tend to speak two languages, the language of criticism and the language of praise. They make a revolting mixture and God wants us to remedy this dualism before we come before him in praise. This is why the psalmist says, 'His praise was on my tongue. If I had cherished sin in my heart, the Lord would not have listened' (Ps 66:17–18).

God wants us to experience his healing and peace in praise, so we must ensure that we keep short accounts with him when it comes to sin. The longer we hold back from exposing our sin to God, the more likely Satan is to trap us in other areas of sin.

All too often, sin prevents people from praising when it shouldn't. So how do we become free of it? Jesus said we find freedom in knowing truth. The truth in this case is, 'If we confess our sins, he is faithful and just and will forgive us our sins' (1 Jn 1:9) because 'the blood of Jesus... purifies us from all sin' (1 Jn 1:7). We will breathe the fresh air of his forgiveness when we agree with this truth.

Guilt feelings

On the day of a trial, it doesn't matter how good the suspect tries to feel, if the judge pronounces him guilty—he is condemned. Similarly, if we are trying to cover up our sin, we also stand in a position of guilt. But once we have made a sincere confession of our sin, God our judge pronounces us forgiven. 'There is now no condemnation for those who are in Christ' (Rom 8:1).

Often, after confessing our sins to God, we can be left with an abstract feeling of guilt lingering on. Our feelings can suggest to us that we're not forgiven, and we begin to wonder whether we actually are. A false sense of guilt has crept in because we have failed to take God at his word.

God never tells us to try and *feel* forgiven, or even to forgive ourselves. He just wants us to believe and trust that we are now 'justified' (Rom 5:9)—just-as-if-I'd never sinned, so that we can 'declare the praises of him who called us out of darkness into his wonderful light' (1 Pet 2:9).

A negative self-image

God sees the people in every meeting as individuals, with individual needs and problems, not as a mass of people crammed together like sardines in a tin. Each one of us is unique in his eyes.

When he created each one of us, you might say he threw away the mould; for every person's face is different. He had only six square inches to work on, and yet no two are identical!

In creating us God was saying something in this universe which he couldn't say other than by bringing us into existence. The realization of his very special love for each one of us can take years to make that important eighteen-inch drop from our heads to our hearts. Here are a few examples of how you can motivate people to reach out and grasp hold of this truth.

The song *Jesus, Take Me As I Am,* where we sing, 'I can come no other way,' can so easily be sung in an attitude of, 'Jesus, leave me as I am, I can be no other way.' It might help if you said a few words about how God wants to rid us of our lack of self-worth by seeing that he values us so much that he died for us. It is at Calvary where we see our true worth.

If you are singing the song *I Receive Your Love,* encourage people to put their hands out in front of them, palms up, as a gesture of actually receiving his love.

Many of us continually wrestle with doubts about whether God really does care for us. Singing 'Jesus, your love has melted my heart' might be more meaningful if you get people to sing 'Jesus, your love is melting my heart.' Many of us need to be released in worship, and as yet we have not allowed the Holy Spirit to melt and permeate the stony areas of our hearts, so we need to sing these words as a prayer of faith.

You could even get just the men to sing the song through, once it's been sung by everybody a few times. To stand back and listen to a bunch of grown men singing such simple yet meaningful words can be a touching experience, especially in our day and age, where showing emotions and feelings so openly is not the done thing.

In the song *I Love You, Lord,* if you sing the last line, 'Let me be a sweet, sweet sound in your ear,' help people to see that we really are a 'sweet, sweet sound' in God's ear and not a dissonance. God wants to make a mighty reversal in the way some of us view ourselves. He wants us to have a holy boldness in singing such words. We can do so because of our relationship to Jesus.

In Zechariah 3, Joshua the high priest is about to worship when Satan begins to accuse him of being unworthy (v.1). If Satan can't deflate with lies, he will try to use truth instead. And the truth of the matter is that without being clothed in Jesus' righteousness, we would be as capable of surviving in God's presence as a piece of paper in the heart of a fire. Jesus' righteousness is the only thing that covers our sin from God's eyes. We can relax in that.

Joshua was obviously relying on his own sense of worth, which is why Satan accused him. Before Joshua could say anything in his own defence, the Lord rebuked Satan (v.2) and then cloaked Joshua's unworthiness with the Lord's righteousness (vv. 3–4).

Joshua then has a mitre put on his head. It's interesting to note that the only way he could have kept it on his head was by holding his head up. Satan tries to get our heads down, accusing us day and night, trying to make us *feel* unworthy so that we end up trying to deserve God's love. He will say, 'What makes you think you can praise? What makes you think you can pray out loud?' Let's not be caught entering into debate with such thoughts. Though Romans 3:10 says, 'There is no-one righteous, not even one,' verse 22 tells us that 'righteousness from God comes through faith in Jesus Christ'. So we should neither abase nor exalt ourselves, nor be caught fighting for ground which Jesus has already won.

Each one of us is intimately related to God and praise can help us 'thaw out' and become more aware of this unique link we have with him, as there is a coming together of our spirit and his.

'And we, who...contemplate the Lord's glory, are being transformed into his likeness' (2 Cor 3:18). Will we dare to believe it?

Wrong concepts of God

When the Bible exhorts us to praise the Lord, what kind of Lord do we have in our minds? Many of us still see God as impersonal, distant, remote and unfeeling, so it is no wonder that coming to pray or sing to him proves to be a task of endurance.

Maybe our experiences with harsh figures of authority have served this image of God in our minds—our teachers, the headmaster, the boss at work, or even our fathers. It is all too easy for us to allow these influences to be superimposed on God whenever we concentrate our minds on him.

If we are to praise him for who he is, we have to make sure we know who he is and who he isn't. He isn't intolerant and easily bored with our company. If we were able momentarily to peep through the safety curtain which hangs between the seen and the unseen world as we pray and sing to God, we wouldn't have to fear that we'd catch him in the act of yawning. Nor do we have to feel that as we come to him with our burdens again and again he grows wearier with each visit. No, he is only hurt when we don't bring our problems to him, for our shoulders were never made to bear the strain of some of the things we carry.

Just as people can be roused and blessed by heartfelt music, so can God. He is thrilled with our praises. If you find that hard to believe, God wants you to know that 'he will rejoice over you with singing' (Zeph 3:17).

Unbelief (doubting what God says) has been described as 'the mother of all sins', and brings all kinds of fears into our lives. Its opposite number, faith (agreeing with what God says), brings a sense of well-being and peace into our hearts. Many of us can spend years being gradually persuaded of God's love for us. But it is when we take up a firm stand on what God says that we will begin to see the reality of his truth being worked out in our lives.

Lack of thought

Some Christians may not tell many lies, but they sing thousands, and thoughtless praise goes no higher than the ceiling. Sometimes, because of over-familiarity with certain hymns and songs, our souls remain untouched in times of singing.

A rather humorous case in point occurred when a bishop was invited to take part in a service at one of the churches in his diocese. He was a man not well acquainted with the use of microphones and, to make matters worse, as he stepped up to speak into the microphone in front of him, it became apparent that it wasn't functioning properly. He quietly said aside to the minister of the church, 'I think there's something wrong with the microphone,' to which the congregation promptly answered, 'And also with you.'

If worship is not a response of our hearts, it will simply become a moving of our lips.

Tradition

We tend to be creatures of habit who don't like too much change, and this can apply to our church life as much as anything. God is a God of order, but we need to understand that he can easily be made a prisoner of too much order and tradition, the attitude which says, 'We've always done it this way, so we always will.'

Maybe we have an inability to receive the new things God has for us because we are harnessed to the old ways of thinking and doing things in our churches. Old wineskins were never meant to hold new wine. Just because God seemed to be saying such-and-such-a-thing from year A to year B, that doesn't necessarily mean he will be saying the same thing to us from year B to year C. He may have moved on, and we have to be willing to move on with him to new pastures.

Most of us will be familiar with the way Lot's wife looked back on her old life in Genesis 19:26. She became what some of our churches are today—lifeless. She became a statue, and if you have ever tried moving a life-size statue, you will know how hard it is to budge. There seems to be a similar sort of resistance in many Christian circles today to the moving of the Holy Spirit, simply because people have become set in their ways. I wonder who presents the greatest problem to God, the backslider or the backsider?

God always has something new to aid us in our enjoyment of him in praise, anything from new songs to new techniques. He wants to give us daily bread to *eat,* not to keep. So sometimes God may give a new song to your fellowship for you to use once, or a few times, so that when it is gone, he can provide you with something else. The important thing is that we are listening expectantly for him to use us as channels of his creativity. One of God's main characteristics is that of a creator, which means that he continues to invent. He could write new songs quite easily by himself: it's just that he wants each one of us, as the hands and feet of his body, to be open to his inspiration. God will enable those he calls.

Reflecting the onward move of God's Spirit among His people, *Songs of Fellowship* is a developing series of worship aids, presenting some of today's most popular songs, mainly from British churches.

The songbooks are designed for church and individual use, and future editions will include a careful selection of new songs as they arise.

Music songbook

Over 150 songs arranged alphabetically by first line for easy use in praise and worship meetings. Fully scored for piano, with guitar chords, and including a full Index and an Index of Scripture References. Available in hardback and wire-o (open-flat) bindings.

Wire-o ISBN 0 86065 117 7
Hardback ISBN 0 86065 160 6

Words-only edition

Wire-stitched with colour covers.
ISBN 0 86065 118 5

Loose-leaf songbook

The complete *Songs of Fellowship* Music Edition with each song on a separate sheet punched to fit standard ring binders, to allow new songs to be inserted as they become available.
ISBN 0 86065 191 6

For overhead projection

The complete *Songs of Fellowship* Words Edition on acetate sheets, for use in public meetings. Supplied in packs of about 85 songs each.

Records and cassettes

The following recordings are available of selected songs, with up to 20 titles on each album.

Volume 1 ☉ KMR 341 ▦ KMC 341
Volume 2 ☉ KMR 345 ▦ KMC 345
Volume 3 ☉ KMR 358 ▦ KMC 358
Volume 4 ☉ KMR 387 ▦ KMC 387
Volume 5 ☉ KMR 388 ▦ KMC 388
Volume 6 ☉ KMR 353 ▦ KMC 353
Volume 7 ☉ KMR 383 ▦ KMC 383
Volume 8 ☉ KMR 404 ▦ KMC 404

Also available on cassette only, *Derek Moon Plays Songs of Fellowship.*
An instrumental medley of 24 of the more popular songs. ▦ KMC 385.

Live worship series

A new series of records and cassettes featuring live praise gatherings from such events as the Downs Bible Week, Spring Harvest, South-and-West Bible Week, and Festival. Some titles are cassette only.

Songs of Fellowship Worship Aids

Teach Yourself Praise Guitar (Book & Cassette)
by Jo King

An invaluable aid to beginners and more established guitarists alike. Jo includes practical hints on how to lead in praise and worship, and demonstrates different strumming techniques to enhance the mood of each song.

Update service

A unique service of loose-leaf music supplements available by post only on annual subscription. Currently the service supplies about eight new songs three times per year. Details from Songs of Fellowship Update Service, P.O. Box 75, Eastbourne, E. Sussex BN23 6NW.

Special projects ministry

Kingsway also help in the preparation of supplementary praise sheets for binding into conference programmes. This includes an extensive copyright clearance service for those who wish to prepare their own material.

All items are published by **Kingsway** and are available from your usual Christian book and record supplier.

Mail Order enquiries to:
Charisma Christian Mail Order,
P.O. Box 75, Eastbourne,
E. Sussex BN23 6NW